Keeping God's Secrets

by
Gwen Shaw

Engeltal Press
P.O. Box 447
Jasper, AR 72641 USA
www.engeltalpress.com

Copyright 2002 by Gwen Shaw
End-Time Handmaidens, Inc.

ISBN 0-9740588-6-6

Printed in the United States of America

KEEPING GOD'S SECRETS
Chapter 1

In Proverbs 25:9b we read, *"discover not a secret to another (Disclose not a secret to another)."*

For years I have felt the importance of teaching God's people that they must learn to keep God's secrets. Many of God's precious revelations cannot be given to us because we are not capable of handling them wisely. We do not have enough reverence and fear of God in our hearts to obey the convictions of our heart. *"The secret of God is with them that fear the Lord."*

The Bible also tells us *"Depart from evil, and do good; and dwell for evermore"* (Psalms 37:27). But sometimes, when we know something and we don't depart from evil, and we don't do good, we will tell it around, and we will bring destruction on another life. In other words, if we hear an evil report about another person, and we talk about it to others (which we will do if we do not have the love and compassion of the Lord in our hearts) we will grieve the Lord, and bring much harm into the life of the individual who has sinned. We may even send them away from God forever, because they will identify God by our actions.

They will believe that if you, a follower of Christ, are cruel and merciless, then your God must also be cruel and merciless.

When the Lord knows that He can trust us with His secrets, He will reveal things to us which He cannot reveal to others.

On the eve before He died, Jesus said to His disciples *"I have yet many things to say unto you, but ye cannot bear them now"* (John 16:12).

The reason that they could not be told these heavenly secrets was because they were not mature enough in the Word of God. It was not because they did not love Jesus — they loved Jesus. They probably loved Him more than you and I. They had lived with Him and knew Him intimately. But they were not mature.

God is going to bring us into a time and place when the secrets that have been sealed up since the days of Daniel, the prophet, shall be revealed. Remember, the Lord speaking to Daniel said to him, *"But thou, O Daniel, shut up the words, and seal the book, even to the time of the end: many shall run to and fro, and knowledge shall be increased"* (Daniel 12:4). The truths that God revealed to Daniel were for another age, and that time is now.

ANGELS KEEP SECRETS

The secrets of God are very precious. When Samson's father, Manoah, was visited by the angel of the Lord, He asked him, *"What is thy name, that when thy sayings come to pass we may do thee honour?"*

The angel replied to him, *"Why askest thou thus after my name, seeing it is secret?"* (Judges 13:17-18).

The angel did not want to reveal his identity because he did not want man to honour him; he wanted all the honour to go to God alone. He was only a messenger of the Lord. Sometimes we honour the messenger more than we honour the ONE who sent him.

The angels minister with pure hearts of love. Much of their ministry is done in secret. They do not publicize their works of love and mercy. They come and go like the wind. They do not ask for recognition or honour. The praises of men mean nothing to them.

END-TIME MINISTRY WILL BE SIMILAR TO THAT OF THE ANGELS

I believe the greatest end-time ministry will be done in secret, just like the angels' ministry is. We will go about unseen, unrecognized, unheralded, and people will wonder who touched them, who helped them, who put that money in their coat pocket, who miraculously delivered them from what would have been a terrible accident, or certain death.

The Holy Ghost has been revealing to saints that we will travel like the wind. The time is going to come when it will be impossible to go to certain places in the natural. Even now, it is practically impossible to get visas for ministry in certain Moslem, Hindu and Communist nations. Air fares are increasingly more expensive — especially if one has to travel at a moment's notice. It is time for us to prepare our hearts for "Philip's Instant Travel." We had better get ready for translation ministries! Glory to God! God did it before, and He can do it again! See Acts 8:39-40, *"And when they were come up out of the water, the Spirit of the Lord caught away Philip, that the eunuch saw him no more: and he went on his way rejoicing. But Philip was found at Azotus: and passing through he preached in all the cities, till he came to Caesarea."* When we have finished our work, delivered our message, the Holy Spirit will catch us away and deliver us to our next appointment. We won't even have time to introduce ourselves, nor will we want to!

"THIRTEEN AT THE TABLE"

Some years ago I came across a wonderful, miraculous testimony in the Assemblies of God weekly magazine, *The Evangel.* It was called "Thirteen At The Table." They gave us permission to use it in our End-Time Handmaiden's Magazine. Later, we invited the writer of that article, the wife of an Assemblies of God preacher, to give her testimony at our 1979 World Convention in Dogpatch, Arkansas. We will never forget it.

Her name was Gladys Triplett. When the miracle visitor came to her house she was living in Newberg, Oregon. Her husband was an ordained minister with the Assemblies of God. They had eight children. The youngest two were sixteen months and three months old. Her husband had gone to another city for revival meetings, leaving her alone with the children. But she was very sick and weak, as she had not recovered fully from the birth of her last child. She had not been able to sleep for some nights. Her house was in a mess, toys scattered everywhere, unmade beds, a mountain of dirty dishes in the sink, and a large pile of dirty laundry waiting for her. After the older children left for school, she sank, exhausted on the couch, only to hear the doorbell ring.

Upon answering it, she found a strange lady standing there, in the pouring rain, who told her that she had come to help her because she had prayed for help.

Gladys sank to her knees, the visitor picked her up, laid her on the couch, telling her, "Sleep now, my child, for He cares for you."

When Gladys woke up three hours later, she found her baby had been freshly bathed and was sleeping in her crib, the older girl was sitting, playing in her high chair, the floor was cleaned, the big pile of laundry was washed, ironed, and put away (even though it was pouring rain and she had no dryer). This was a task that usually took her more than two days in good weather. The dishes were washed, dinner was ready, including a newly baked cake, and the table was set with her best linen for thirteen people. Gladys tried to find out who the kind helper was, but she only answered, "a friend, a child of God." She said she had been sent by the Father, Who loved her and had heard her cry for help in the night.

Gladys told her that there wouldn't be thirteen for supper, as her husband was gone, and they didn't have that many children. But she answered, that there would be thirteen for dinner. Sure enough, her husband arrived, saying his meeting had been cancelled, and he brought five guests with him. There were thirteen at the table, and the little girl in her high chair. While they were eating, the visitor washed all the pots and pans, and when Gladys went into the kitchen, she was gone. They inquired if any of the neighbours, or even the police might know who she was, but no one knew anything about her. She was simply, "a friend, a child of God" who, as she had told Gladys, when asked how she got there, answered, "As a crow flies, so came I."

Upon closer inspection, she discovered that all the children's newly-laundered clothes were in their correct drawers. Who but an angel would know what belonged to whom!

I believe that, even as the angels worked with the saints in the Bible, they will work with us today. In fact, if we had eyes to see them, we would find that they are all around us. Many times people have seen angels when I have been ministering the Word of God. Angels will work with us, and we will work with them through our prayers which will give them strength to fight against the demons. We are going to join the angels in their ministry and they are going to work with us. It is going to be "the angel together with the saints ministry" of the end-time. Are you getting ready for it?

Chapter 2

PAUL'S SECRET

Even now, the Lord is doing wonderful things which His children are forbidden to talk about. Paul had experiences which he only referred to slightly as having been caught up into paradise and hearing *"unspeakable words, which it is not lawful for a man to utter"* (2 Corinthians 12:4).

Sometimes we wonder why God does not let us tell all the good things that are revealed to us. But we must remember Jesus often warned people to keep things secret.

In Hebrews 5:11-14, Paul said that he had many things which he wanted to teach the Church, but they were not able to receive that teaching now because they were incapable of understanding deeper truths. They were still babes who only wanted milk (simple, easy-to-understand stories), and had no appetite for the real meat of the Word. Sad to say, there are many revelations and Heavenly truths which Paul never shared. They remained "God's secrets." We are the poorer because of that. I believe that there are many prophets and seers in the Church who know some of these secrets, but refuse to share them because they know they will not be understood.

PETER'S SECRET

When Peter made the great confession, *"Thou art the Christ, the Son of the living God,"* Jesus told him that he had received this great revelation from His Father in Heaven. He said, that upon this truth, He would build His Church. As they were leaving the place of revelation, Jesus charged His disciples that they should tell no man that He was Jesus the Christ (Matthew 16:20). That was a pretty difficult secret for the disciples to keep.

PETER, JAMES AND JOHN HAD A SECRET

One of the greatest experiences Peter, James and John had is called, "The Transfiguration of Christ." It took place on a mountain. No one had ever experienced anything like that before. It was absolutely sensational, and if news of it had gotten around, people would have gone mad. They wouldn't have let Jesus out of their eyesight, day or night. But what did Jesus say to His three disciples who experienced this phenomenon? On the way down the mountain He warned them, *"Tell the vision to no man, until the Son of man be risen again from the dead"* (Matthew 17:9).

JESUS HEALED A DEAF MAN AND TOLD HIM TO KEEP IT SECRET

One day, when Jesus was at Galilee, they brought to him a man who was deaf, and had an impediment in his speech, in the hope that Jesus would heal him. The Gospel says that Jesus, *"took him aside from the multitude, and put His fingers into his ears, and He spit, and touched his tongue; And looking up to heaven, He sighed, and saith unto him, Ephphatha, that is, Be opened. And straightway his ears were opened, and the string of his tongue was loosed, and he spake plain. And He charged them that they should tell no man: but the more He charged them, so much the more a great deal they published it; And were beyond measure astonished, saying, He hath done all things well: He maketh both the deaf to hear, and the dumb to speak"* (Mark 7:33-37).

JESUS HEALS A BLIND MAN SECRETLY AND TELLS HIM TO KEEP IT A SECRET UNTIL HE GOT BACK TO HIS HOUSE

At Bethsaida the people brought a blind man to Jesus for healing. He took him by the hand, led him out of the town, and when He had spit on his eyes, He put his hands upon him, He asked the man if he saw anything. The man, looking up, said, *"I see men as trees, walking."* The second time, Jesus put His hands upon his eyes, and told him to look. This time the man's sight was completely restored. He could see clearly. Jesus sent him away to his home, saying, *"Neither go into the town, nor tell it to any in the town"* (Mark 8:26).

Why did Jesus warn the man to go straight home to his family and not stop to talk to people on the way? It could have been because people would have questioned him, rebuked him and doubted his testimony. Perhaps the man was still weak in faith. It had taken two touches of Jesus' hands to heal him, and he had not come of his own accord to Jesus.

Someone else had brought him. Apparently, it wasn't the man's faith that had healed him, it was his friend's faith, working together with Jesus' faith, that had brought about this miracle.

Sometimes when we try to tell someone who is a cynic and a doubter about our miracle, the devil will use that one to rob us of our miracle. There are times when we are even forbidden to bear witness of a miracle until our faith is strong enough to stand the testings of the unbelievers who will mock us and doubt our experience. Jesus knew that the enemy would raise up too many who would be antagonists against the Lord of Glory.

WHY WAS THE LEPER WHO WAS HEALED TOLD TO SHOW HIMSELF TO THE PRIEST?

Luke tells us that one day, as Jesus was approaching a city, a certain man who was "full of leprosy" saw Jesus walking by. He fell on his face, and begged Him, *"Lord, if Thou wilt, Thou canst make me clean."* Jesus *"put forth His hand, and touched him, saying, I will: be thou clean. And immediately the leprosy departed from him."* Suddenly, that horribly deformed man, who must have been a sickening sight, was made absolutely whole. Can you imagine the joy, the amazement, the wonder of it all! Anyone standing by must have let out screams of delight. But Jesus *"charged him to tell no man: but go, and shew thyself to the priest, and offer for thy cleansing, according as Moses commanded, for a testimony unto them."* Jesus was doing what the Torah had commanded.

The last man was permitted to go straight home to his house. But the leper could not go to his house until he was pronounced clean by the priests. Only then was he free to return to his family.

It is impossible to keep a miracle secret, so every time another miracle happened the fame of Jesus spread around the country, until everyone was talking about Him (Luke 5:12-15).

KEEP THE RESURRECTION OF JAIRUS' DAUGHTER A SECRET

When the daughter of Jairus, the ruler of the synagogue, was dying, her father came to find Jesus to bring Him to his house to heal his daughter. But before Jesus got there, the child had already died, and the mourners had gathered for the wake. Their loud wails and their unbelief hindered them from seeing a great miracle. Jesus knew they were full of unbelief. They didn't even want to see a miracle. Their hearts were hard, even though they seemed to be weeping. But they only wept because they were hired, professional mourners and got paid for their job. If there was no funeral, they wouldn't get their salary. They rejoiced every time there was a funeral, and they were called to perform. They mocked Jesus when He said the child was "sleeping."

Jesus took the girl's parents into the room where the child lay, and commanded all the mourners to leave the room. He took the girl by her hand and called, *"Maid, arise."* When she came to life there was great joy in that room. But Jesus charged the parents that they should tell no man what had truly happened. He let the people think that they had made a mistake, she had only been sleeping! The mourners didn't get their pay that day! Neither did they see one of the greatest of our Lord's miracles. And Jairus and his wife couldn't even talk about it to anyone! Another reason Jesus told the parents to keep it secret was because of who Jairus was. He was the leader of the local synagogue, a man of high position. If he would have confessed openly to the miracle, he would have been thrown out of his own synagogue. Jesus didn't want this to happen. He needed to keep the man in a place of authority where he could help the people to draw closer to God .

Don't think that you have to tell everybody everything that the Lord does for you! There is a time when silence is expedient. Don't give the devil an opportunity to mock what God has done. Don't cast your pearls to the swine! (Matthew 7:6).

JESUS BEFORE THE SANHEDRIN

When Jesus was brought before the Sanhedrin the chief priests questioned him, *"Art thou the Christ? Tell us."* Jesus knew that they wouldn't believe it if He told them the truth about Himself. He answered them, *"If I tell you, ye will not believe."*

But when they commanded Jesus to answer them in the name of God, He was compelled to give them an answer. His answer is very powerful. *"And he said unto them, 'Ye say that I am'"* (Luke 22:70).

By their deeds, they were fulfilling the prophetic Scriptures. They were performing the very things that the prophets had said they would do to the Messiah.

They, themselves, by their rejection of Him, were bearing witness that He was The Christ, the King of the Jews.

Chapter 3

SPIES MUST OPERATE IN SECRET

Before Joshua led the armies of Israel into the Promised Land, he sent two men to spy out the Land. Their mission was a secret one. A spy is someone who knows how to keep his mouth shut. I believe, as we are coming into this end-time, we will have to learn how to move in secrecy if we are going to conquer the enemy and redeem the land.

There is power in secrecy, because the enemy cannot make use of information to destroy God's plan. God will not trust you to handle underground ministries until you know how to die for the sake of a secret.

Many of our brothers and sisters are tortured in Persecuted Lands because they refuse to reveal the names of their fellow Christians. Their tormenters lie to them and promise them that if they will reveal those who are Christians that they will not be tortured any more, and will be set free. But those honourable men and women of God know that if they betray their brothers and sisters in Christ, they too would be persecuted, and may even have to die at the hands of those who hate Christ. So they remain silent under great duress, and they usually have to pay a terrible price.

THE IMPORTANCE OF KEEPING A SECRET

Job says that even in his youth he knew how to keep the secrets of God. Is that the thing that made Job great? Job says, *"As I was in the days of my youth, when the secret of God was upon my tabernacle"* (Job 29:4).

Job sees himself as the Lord's tabernacle, which hid the Lord's secret. Do you remember what the Holy of Holies was? It was a secret place separated from the Holy Place by a thick, heavy veil. The priests of Israel were forbidden to pass beyond that veil. Only the High Priest could enter, and then it was only on the Day of Atonement. What was the mystery about that Holy of Holies? What made it so holy?

It was the beautiful golden Ark of the Covenant, wherein the Holy Torah was kept. No man dared look upon it with his eyes. When it was moved about it was always wrapped up so that no one could see it. What happened when some men dared to look into the Ark of the Covenant? They were smitten dead. 1 Samuel 6:19 tells us that 50,070 men died because they broke the Holy Law of keeping God's secret thing secret.

Beloved, God was already trying to prepare an elect company by teaching them the importance of secret warfare, secret worship, secret knowledge in God. God said you can not look into the Holy of Holies unless you are qualified for high priesthood ministry. Today we are the Tabernacle of the Lord, and the Ark of the Covenant dwells in our hearts. The secret of the Lord is in our tabernacle. Sad to say, that in some lives, the Holy Presence of God is so covered with sin and debris, unbelief and wrong teaching, that the gold never shines out to the world.

THERE IS SUPERNATURAL PROTECTION IN THE SECRET PLACE

Psalm 27:5 says, *"For in the time of trouble He shall hide me in His pavilion: in the secret of His tabernacle shall He hide me; He shall set me up upon a rock."* That means that there is a covering, there is a storm shelter, an air raid shelter, a shelter where neither chemical, biological nor nuclear weapon can harm me. I thank God that we have such a secret tabernacle! The secret of the Lord is revealed to those that fear Him, and He hides them in the secret (mystic) depth of His Tabernacle. I know that if I am in that Tabernacle there will be an ample, miraculous supply of oxygen because He made the oxygen. When He created Adam, He breathed oxygen into his nostrils, thereby giving him life. God still has His oxygen supply!

ABRAHAM, THE FRIEND OF GOD

Abraham was a man who could keep God's secrets. In Genesis 22 we read the account of how Abraham was commanded by the Lord to offer up his son, Isaac, as a sacrifice. Josephus, in his *History of the Jews*, tells that Abraham did not tell Sarah what he was intending to do. He kept it secret from her. If she would have known his intentions she would have fought Abraham with every ounce of strength in her body. And Isaac, seeing how distressed his mother was, would have refused to submit to this testing. Josephus says that Abraham did not tell Sarah lest he be hindered from obeying God.

Sometimes, if you reveal the leading of God in your life to your family or dearest friends, they will do everything they can to hinder you because they want to spare you pain.

Abraham wasn't God's friend by accident; he was God's friend because friends share secrets they don't divulge to others. Friends have secrets they don't even tell their parents, their children or their spouses. Don't believe that you have to tell your spouse everything. If you are an Abraham you don't tell your wife God's secrets, or His demands on your life. You are free to make sacrifices which she need not know about; and this is true of the wife also.

Micah 7:5 says, *"Trust ye not in a friend, put ye not confidence in a guide: keep the doors of thy mouth from her that lieth in thy bosom."* And then it goes on to tell you why—*"For the son dishonoureth the father, the daughter riseth up against her mother, the daughter-in-law against her mother-in-law; a man's enemies are the men of his own house"* (Micah 7:6).

Abraham's dearest love, Sarah, could have been his enemy if he had said to her, "Sarah I am going to go and offer Isaac as a sacrifice." God could trust Abraham to know His secret plans to pour out His wrath on Sodom and Gomorrah. Remember when the Lord went to visit Abraham, He said, *"Shall I hide from Abraham that thing which I do; Seeing that Abraham shall surely become a great and mighty nation, and all the nations of the earth shall be blessed in him?"* (Genesis 18:17-18).

The secret of the Lord is with the prophets of the Lord. The Lord has given them inner wisdom and knowledge that is absolutely tremendous. Amos 3:7 says, *"Surely the Lord GOD will do nothing, but he revealeth his secret unto his servants the prophets."*

When the Lord gives you "marching orders," or shares with you the secrets of His heart, keep it to yourself. Be careful what you share with others. Sometimes even your dear friend can turn against you. The Holy Spirit may plant a heavenly secret in you which He didn't plant in your friend because that one is not ready for it yet. Don't share it with that one, because the devil can take that beautiful, precious truth and twist it, working on their minds to cause agitation against you to such a degree that it will become an offense — a rock of stumbling. Don't take it for granted that everyone is going to believe your "heavenly-secrets," visions and revelations. By sharing your secret you could even cause them to sin against the Holy Ghost.

Also, you could be guilty of aborting the plan of God. What is an abortion? Abortion is bringing to the world what is not ready for birth. There are abortions which are not intentional. We call them a miscarriage. They are not purposely induced. A spiritual abortion is the birthing of an undeveloped plan. It has not been matured enough to be able to survive. If you begin to divulge the secrets of God to someone who has not yet heard from God themselves, that one will run with it and destroy themselves and others with that very thing that could later have been to the salvation and help of multitudes of people. They will also be likely to destroy you! I believe that, as we are coming to this end-time, we are going to have to learn how to be wise concerning the secrets of God, lest we be hindered from obeying God.

JACOB ESCAPES IN SECRET

In Genesis 31:20 we read, *"And Jacob stole away unawares to Laban the Syrian, in that he told him not that he fled."*

Jacob was the grandson of Abraham. He was living with his father-in-law Laban, who was a Syrian. He had served Laban for twenty years; and at the end of all those difficult years he realized that if he did not steal away, he would never be able to leave. He had already seen the hate Laban had for him in his eyes. The whole family had turned against him. God had spoken to him to return home to his father's house. He knew he had to go, but he knew that Laban was capable of using force to prevent him from leaving. Not only was the flock he had obtained through hard labour in danger of being confiscated by Laban, even his life, and the lives of his family were not safe any more. He knew that if he was to leave, he would have to do it secretly. He waited for an opportunity to get out when it was safe. That chance came when Laban and his sons were in distant pastures with the sheep. Jacob moved quickly, taking his family and sheep with him.

Now, don't you decide to pack your suitcase and run away! You have to know beyond a shadow of a doubt that there is no other way that you can live and serve God. First, fast and pray over your situation. If your life is in danger you may have to flee suddenly, but if you are still safe in the circumstances, I admonish you to fast a prophet-length fast for your situation to change. Then, if it doesn't change and God releases you or commands you to go, (like He did Jacob) then you must obey God to be in His will. This is something you have to feel by the sweet Spirit of God down deep in your soul.

Chapter 4

JOSEPH

The third of the patriarchs we want to mention is Joseph, the son of Jacob and Rachel. The secret of God came upon Joseph's tabernacle when he was seventeen years old. At that time the revelations of God and secrets concerning his future were given to him, but he didn't have the maturity to keep them secret, and that is what got Joseph into all of his troubles. He went around telling his brothers, "I had a dream last night, boys. I sure had a dream. God loves me, and you had better watch out because I am going to be famous one day. I am going to have a big name for myself. My father and mother and all of you are going to recognize that I am special."

Beloved, you may one day be "special" also, but you need to recognize you will only be special by the grace and the goodness of God.

And yet, the wonderful thing was that even though he was a fool and told the secret, and got himself in trouble; because he was sorry and cried out to the Lord from the pit, the Lord took his mistakes and worked them for good.

God could have put Joseph in that place of authority without the pit experience because He can do anything. God is getting us ready for Millennium

Kingdom reigning, and we will need to go through tribulation if we are not ready for it. We can only go through the trials that are coming upon this world through the power of an anointed life. If we are not ready for what is coming, God will put us in the "pressure-cooker," so that we will have the qualification for greatness. God knows how to work in all of our lives.

We know that later in his life Joseph learned to keep his secrets, because when his brothers came to Egypt to buy grain he hid his identity from them. Genesis 42:6-7 says, *"And Joseph was the governor over the land, and he it was that sold to all the people of the land: and Joseph's brethren came, and bowed down themselves before him with their faces to the earth. And Joseph saw his brethren, and he knew them, but made himself strange unto them."*

When he saw his brothers, did he say, "I am Joseph — now I've got you in my hands!"? What did he do? He kept his identity secret, and by keeping the secret he was able to do what he had to do to bless his family. There was still a work of processing that the Holy Ghost had to do in all their lives and especially in the heart of Simeon. He had been the most cruel to Joseph, and the only way God could break old Simeon down was to send him to jail. God broke him in the prison. God had to take that last trace of meanness out of that man, and He did it, because Joseph could keep a secret.

When we can keep a secret through the anointing, God can take the meanness out of that mean

"Simeon" in our families. Some of you women suffer persecution from your husbands because you don't want to keep your mouth shut. You let them listen to tapes they have no business listening to. You leave books lying around which their unregenerate souls are totally incapable of understanding. Or you tell them the secrets of God that you hear in your bedroom chamber. They are not ready for it. God has to put your "Simeon" in jail first. He has to put him in a place where He can break his rebellious will. And **you** have to wait!

Another very enlightening thing that Joseph did took place when his family moved to Egypt. He told his brothers that when Pharaoh asks them about what their trade was, they should not confess to being shepherds, instead they were to say they were cattlemen. This was because sheep were considered unclean to the Egyptians, and to be a shepherd was an abomination. Josephus writes that the Egyptians were forbidden to have anything to do with sheep. There is a reason for that, but we do not want to go into that now.

As you serve the Lord and travel to nations where you are forbidden to preach the Gospel, you will fill out many forms that will include the question, "What is your occupation?" Don't think that you have to be so honest that you should write "minister of the Gospel." or missionary, or evangelist, etc. You will close the door to yourself. Instead, you can honestly tell them you are a teacher, or a housewife, or retired. How do you think we went back and forth across the Iron Curtain borders during those years we smuggled

Bibles into Eastern Europe? Be wise as a serpent, and harmless as a dove! Because his brothers took his advice, Joseph was able to locate them in the best pasture land of Egypt.

God is going to put us in the best place in the kingdom, He has a divine plan for us. King Jesus has gone ahead of us. He says, "I prepared all these things for you and I am going to give you the best of the land, but keep your mouth shut. I have a work for you to do but you must know how to keep My secrets."

THE MIDWIVES' SECRET

We read an amazing story about the midwives who saved the lives of the newly-born boy babies of the Hebrew women in Egypt (Exodus 1:16-21). God established these holy women, these wise women. The king had given command that all boy babies born to the Hebrew women must be instantly put to death. But the godly midwives refused to obey the king's orders. Because they saved so many lives, God honored them and "gave them houses," or, gave them greatness in His Kingdom. These women knew how to keep a secret that a boy-baby had been born.

We are in the business of delivering the "man-child." We must learn to keep our mouths shut. Don't go around telling everyone that you are expecting the "man-child" to be born. Too many already think they are Elijah. The "man-child" is being born, but in secret, in great secrecy, without a lot of bragging, without a lot of boasting, and without a "holier than thou" spirit. The spiritual midwives were raised up of God to secretly go from house to house to deliver those little baby boys. Those babies were the future hope of Israel. They would lead the tribes to warfare and victory, and they would be there in the wilderness where God would reveal to them many of His wonders.

One of those little babies that were saved was Moses. His mother's name was Jochebed. Jochebed did not obey the king; she made a little ark; she got the revelation from the story of how Noah built the ark. He saved his family. She had faith to save her son. She lined it with pitch and put it in the Nile river with all the crocodiles, but she knew that she had a God in Heaven Who was able to protect her baby. There aren't enough "crocodiles" to eat the "man-child." She went home to pray, while she sent that "junior handmaiden" (Miriam) down to the river to watch and see what God would do. She was but a girl, but she was not too young to know the importance of keeping a secret.

Sometimes, as parents, we have to go and hide, and let the kids do the job. God is raising up our youth. They may be the ones who will save our lives tomorrow.

Bless her heart, that little Miriam could keep her mouth shut, too. She saw the king's daughter come down to the river to bathe in the waters. When the princess found her "baby in a basket," Miriam ran up to her and offered to find her a wet nurse. She didn't say, "I'll go and get Mama — she knows how to nurse our brother so he won't cry." She knew how to keep a secret. Oh, the wisdom in Miriam's heart! How could that child learn to keep silence? Because in tribulation you will learn to keep your mouth shut.

Chapter 5

RAHAB

All nations have spies. In Bible times, Israel also had spies. Joshua, the commander of Israel's armies, decided to send two spies into the Land of Canaan to spy out the land so they could determine its strength. These two spies came to Rahab the harlot's house (Joshua 2:14). Through her they were able to learn the thoughts of the enemy, because Rahab said the whole land is trembling in fear of you.

It is so important that we know in this hour where to hide—it might not be in the house of a Christian, it might be in a harlot's house! They were in danger of being discovered while on their secret mission, and it was a good place to hide! Their lives were "on the line." They knew that if Rahab couldn't keep a secret they would be arrested and put to death. They had to trust her. What she told them gave them the faith they needed. Now they knew for sure that God was going to give them the city of Jericho, and all the land. They realized that the warfare would be intense, that many would die, for God had commanded them to spare no lives. On the other hand, they were indebted to Rahab for sparing their lives when the soldiers came to her house looking for them. So they agreed to spare her life and the lives of her loved ones because of her kindness to them.

If we can keep a secret we will not only save our own lives, we will also save the lives of those we love. I believe if we will learn how to keep secrets in the next few years we will be able to save many lives. I believe we will be given the opportunity to save those who are in danger because of antisemitism and persecution. We will have to have hiding places, like Corrie Ten Boom did, for those who are fleeing for their lives. We have to learn how to save both Jews and Christians. Again in our land there will be a secret Underground Railroad like our forefathers had when they tried to assist the Negro slaves who attempted to escape from their cruel masters. The abolitionists who were caught helping them were punished severely, so once again, many will lay their lives down to save others.

The same happened in the days of Hitler's rule in Germany. All who saved the lives of the Jews did it knowing that their lives were in great danger, for if they were caught it meant sure death. But they were organized. We learned from others how to save lives. Everyone should read *The Hiding Place*, the story of how one brave family in Amsterdam saved the lives of many Jews.

Rahab saved the lives of those two spies, and they saved her life in the day of war, when the city was condemned to be destroyed—all because they knew how to keep a secret. It's the old Law of God, A LIFE FOR A LIFE!

SAMSON

Samson was a man who could not keep a secret, even though his life depended on it. He had the anointing, he had the power of God, he had the deliverance ministry, but he put his head on the lap of the wicked and traitorous Delilah once too often! God's people must be careful where they lay their heads! We must never rest in false comfort. The Word of God warns us, *"Trust ye not in a friend, put ye not confidence in a guide: keep the doors of thy mouth from her that lieth in thy bosom"* (Micah 7:5). But Samson did not heed this godly warning, and when Delilah repeatedly begged him to tell her what was the secret of his great strength, he pushed from his conscience the warning of God that he must always keep this secret in his heart. He broke down and told her "all his heart" — *"if I be shaven, then my strength will go from me, and I shall become weak, and be like any other man."* As a result, while he was sleeping, she called his enemies, and they cut off his hair, leaving him in a state of weakness. When he was without strength they blinded him, and made him their slave.

If we do not heed the warning of God and keep His secrets, we too can become slaves of those who hate us. Many Christians think that the devil knows everything. That is not true. He is NOT omniscient. The devil knows a lot; he has a lot demons and people working for him, but he doesn't know it all, unless we tell him. If we keep our mouths shut, the demons are not going to be able to report to the devil our thoughts, because they do not know them. It wasn't until the demon in Delilah found out the secret, that he could tell it to Samson's enemies. If the devil would have known it sooner, all he would have had to do was tell his fortune tellers and soothsayers the secret of Samson's strength, and he would have been destroyed earlier. There are a lot of things the devil still does not know.

Sometimes I am surprised, when I have been on dangerous secret missions for the Lord, how little the enemies of the Lord know. God keeps them in a state of confusion. They know a lot, but they still don't know everything. We have to risk that chance that they don't know. You have to believe God in the dangerous and evil days that lie ahead of us that He will cover our tracks, and hide us in His secret pavilion.

When Samson told the secret of his anointing, he lost his power. If you tell all the good secrets of God's anointing in your life, you are a fool. You don't need to tell where you got the anointing! How can I tell what made me until I tell what suffering I went through? How can I tell the suffering I went through if I don't tell who made me suffer? How can I not tell who made me suffer without pointing my finger and destroying somebody's reputation, and robbing them of the little honour they still have? And how can I hurt their family and relatives who still are living?

There is a time coming when all things will be revealed, but until then, keep even your enemy's identity secret. Your enemy could be another Christian. And to reveal your enemy's evil ways would bring dishonour to our Lord Jesus. When the enemy of the Christians discover the sins which a child of God has committed, he will bring shame to all of us who love the Lord. Then the evil one laughs at us and mocks us to scorn.

When Saul and his sons were killed on the battlefront, David said, *"Tell it not in Gath, publish it not in the streets of Askelon; lest the daughters of the Philistines rejoice, lest the daughters of the uncircumcised triumph"* (2 Samuel 1:20). Many have lost their vision because they couldn't keep their mouths shut.

RUTH

When Naomi instructed Ruth how to present her need to Boaz (Ruth 3:1-14), the entire proceedings were enacted in secret. Naomi told her to act in secret, and Boaz told her to *"Let it not be known that a woman came into the floor"* (verse 14). We have to be careful of the appearance of evil, because we can destroy the weak consciences of other people who cannot understand a situation. Ruth obeyed her mother-in-law's wise advice because she knew the customs of the people. Everything must be done in secret. If it had been made known to the neighbours, it could have turned into a terrible situation which would have destroyed the whole plan of God for the House of Judah. There are things that God calls us to do that we can only do in the dark. If it had not been for the hours of darkness there is no way that we could have succeeded in our Underground Ministry in the Iron Curtain nations. We waited until it was dark before we started moving out to visit the secret Christians. If we had tried to do it in the daylight, it would have, not only have been dangerous for us, it would have been even more dangerous for them. Thank God, He gives us a "cloak of darkness" to help us to do good deeds also.

Why did Boaz tell Ruth to keep her visit to him a secret? He knew that both he and she would have lost their honour. Sometimes things have to be done in secret lest those who are God's chosen people lose their honour before the world. You know what you are doing is not wrong, and I know it is all right. Our consciences are clean before God, but we have to be careful that we do not bring reproach upon the Lord, nor endanger others.

SAMUEL'S ANOINTING OF DAVID

When God wanted Samuel to anoint the shepherd boy, David, to be the next king of Israel, He told him, *"How long wilt thou mourn for Saul, seeing I have rejected him from reigning over Israel? fill thine horn with oil, and go, I will send thee to Jesse the Bethlehemite: for I have provided me a king among his sons. And Samuel said, How can I go? if Saul hear it, he will kill me. And the LORD said, Take an heifer with thee, and say, I am come to sacrifice to the LORD. And call Jesse to the sacrifice, and I will shew thee what thou shalt do: and thou shalt anoint unto me him whom I name unto thee"* (1 Samuel 16:1-3).

The Lord said to Samuel, don't tell them what you are going to do, because Saul has his spies all over the land and they are going to find out, then your life, and the lives of the family of Jesse, will be in danger. Who did the people of the land watch more than Samuel?

When Samuel moved, it was like the king moved. Everybody watched what Samuel did, and it was reported right away to King Saul who was full of suspicion and hated anyone who might prove to be a threat to his throne.

So God told him to take his heifer with him to the house of Jesse in Bethlehem, then when people asked him what he was doing, he could honestly say that God had called him to offer a sacrifice in Bethlehem. Some might say, "But that is acting out a lie." God gave him a plan which would allow him to tell enough of the truth to satisfy the curious without having to lie.

It is about time you learn a little bit of the art of covering your tracks. God gives His people wisdom and knowledge. Be wise as a serpent as well as harmless as a dove. Samuel would have never been able to anoint David if he had not done it the right way, the secret way.

Chapter 6

WHY DO WE WANT TO KNOW GOD'S SECRETS?

If you want to know God's secrets, as most of us do, it is because we were created to know the deeper things of God. There will always be a void in our souls until we become intimate with God, as our father Adam and our mother Eve were, who walked and talked with God every day, learning from Him continually. But God knows that since sin entered the world, we are not able to receive and understand many of the secret things of God, because we have not reached the state of "grace" which they were in already.

While they were still in the state of innocence, God said to them, *"But of the tree of the knowledge of good and evil, thou shalt not eat of it: for in the day that thou eatest thereof thou shalt surely die"* (Genesis 2:17).

Adam and Eve were tempted by the thought of being able to know the secrets of God so that they could be equal with Him. It would be wonderful if we could be as wise as God, but then we would also have to be omniscient, omnipotent, omnipresent and perfect in love. If we had all wisdom and power, and not perfect love, we would destroy others with our knowledge and power. Paul said, *"And though I... understand all mysteries, and all knowledge...and have not love, I am nothing"* (1 Corinthians 13:2). That is why it is so important that when we know God's secrets, we should also know how to **keep** God's secrets.

Deuteronomy 29:29 says, *"The secret things belong unto the Lord our God: but those things which are revealed belong unto us and to our children forever, that we may do all the words of this Law."* It is one thing to have the Word of God on the walls of your house, but its another thing to have them written on the walls of your heart.

SECRET MINISTRIES

Some of the greatest ministries that are going to be done in the end-time are going to be done anonymously. God wants to prepare us for them. When you do something anonymously there is no pride attached because you are not getting recognition or fame — no one knows you were the one who gave that large sum of money, or who showed mercy to another person in need. The Good Samaritan was nameless.

Job was a secret philanthropist, he said, in Job 29:4, *"The secret of the Lord is upon my tabernacle."*

HOW TO DISCOVER THE SECRETS OF GOD

The Psalmist says in Psalm 25:14, *"The secret of the Lord is with them that fear Him."* Psalm 27:5 says, *"In the secret of His tabernacle shall He hide me."* In Psalm 91:1 we read, *"He that dwelleth in the secret place of the most High shall abide under the shadow of the Almighty."* As these dark days are coming upon us we will have to draw very close to the Lord, and live in that intimate relationship with Him, where we will have "around the clock" protection.

IN THE SECRET PLACE OF THE STAIRS

There is a place in God where only those who have a great hunger for God make every effort to climb higher and higher.

The Beloved of the Song of Solomon calls to His bride, *"O my dove, that art in the clefts of the rock, in the secret places of the stairs, let me see thy countenance, let me hear thy voice; for sweet is thy voice, and thy countenance is comely"* (Song of Solomon 2:14).

The cleft of the Rock is where God hides Himself when He wants to meet with His beloved, this is the place He promised to meet with Moses when Moses longed for His glorious Presence.

When Moses besought God, *"Show me thy glory!"* The Lord answered him, *"There is a place here by me, and thou shalt stand upon a rock; And it shall come to pass, while my glory passeth by, that I will put thee in a cleft of the rock, and I will cover thee with My hand while I pass by"* (Exodus 33:18, 21-22).

In the "Rock of Ages" there is a cleft where the spear was driven into the side of Jesus. If you hide yourself in the side of Jesus, right underneath that rib, you will know all the secrets of eternity that He has saved in His heart to share with you when you are ready for them. You can go right into the heart of that Rock, and you can have a revelation in God that is beyond the limitations of the natural. The veil will be removed so that you can see and know as you are seen and known.

DANIEL

One of the saints of God, who had a key to the secrets of God, was Daniel the prophet. He had a tremendous open door to the secrets of God.

When King Nebuchadnezzar had a dream which he could not remember, but which he felt was of utmost importance, he called in his magicians and astrologers and Chaldeans to tell him what the dream had been, and give the interpretation. They were baffled by such a demand. They said to the king, *"There is none other that can show it before the king, except the gods, whose dwelling is not with flesh."* In his fury, the king demanded that all his wise men be slain. But when Daniel was told about the king's decision, he went to prayer, and God gave him the answer in a dream, *"Then was the secret revealed unto Daniel in a night vision. Then Daniel blessed the God of heaven"* (Daniel 2:19).

Nebuchadnezzar, upon seeing this great gift in Daniel, fell upon his face and worshipped, saying, *"Of a truth it is, that your God is a God of gods, and a Lord of kings, and a revealer of secrets, seeing thou couldest reveal this secret"* (Daniel 2:47). God is going to have a people like Daniel in these days!

Later, when Daniel was an old man, Nebuchadnezzar's grandson, Belshazzar, the king, on the eve of the destruction of the Babylonian Kingdom, made a great feast for all his lords. In a drunken state he called for the vessels of the Holy Temple, which had been brought to Babylon when Jerusalem was sacked, so that they could drink their wine from them. This was a sacrilegious act because they had been dedicated to the Lord God, Jehovah. Man must never use these holy vessels in a profane way. The crowd drank wine, and praised the gods of gold and silver, etc. In the same hour there appeared a man's hand, and it began to write a message on the wall of the palace that they could not understand. Everyone began to tremble with fear. The most terrified of all was the king, himself. He called for his wise men to give him the interpretation of these words. But they too did not know the answer.

Then the queen mother, upon hearing what had happened, came to the great hall and announced to the king, *"There is a man in thy kingdom, in whom is the spirit of the holy gods; and in the days of thy father light and understanding and wisdom, like the wisdom of the gods, was found in him; whom the king Nebuchadnezzar thy father, the king, I say, thy father, made master of the magicians, astrologers, Chaldeans, and soothsayers; Forasmuch as an excellent spirit, and knowledge, and understanding, interpreting of dreams, and shewing of hard sentences, and dissolving of doubts, were found in the same Daniel, whom the king named Belteshazzar: now let Daniel be called, and he will shew the interpretation"* (Daniel 5:11-12).

When Daniel appeared, the king begged him, trembling, *"I have heard of thee, that thou canst make interpretations, and dissolve doubts: now if thou canst read the writing, and make known to me the interpretation thereof, thou shalt be clothed with scarlet, and have a chain of gold about thy neck, and shalt be the third ruler in the kingdom"* (Daniel 5:16).

Not only could Daniel read the words on the wall, he was able to give the interpretation of them. He could do it because God gave him the secret meaning of the words. It was a very dire warning that the end had come for the Babylonian Kingdom. That night, the city of Babylon fell to the Persians and most of the people who had been at that feast were put to death. But God had warned them through the Prophet whom the Lord God could trust with His secrets.

There was no secret that could be hidden from Daniel. King Nebuchadnezzar had given him the title, "Master of Magicians." That was the only way he could describe his ability to know secret things. They believed in magicians but they did not understand about holy prophecy or seers. God's seers could see beyond the natural realm into the spiritual secrets of God. God gave Daniel revelation in the secret visions of the night.

It is in the night vigils that the secret revelations of God will be given to you. In the "dark night of the soul" when you are going through trials and great testings and the way before you is hidden in darkness, the greatness of God will be revealed to you.

Later, God gave Daniel all the secrets of the end-time, and then God said to him in Daniel 12:4, *"Shut up the words, and seal the book, even to the time of the end: many shall run to and fro, and knowledge shall be increased."*

It will only be those who have the same anointing as Daniel who will be able to rightly interpret the end-time scriptures that concern the eschatology of the times. Many try to understand it. They use mathematics and their knowledge of the Scriptures, and still they miss it. Some have made drastic mistakes when they have attempted to prophecy the dates of the coming of the Lord. Only the "Daniels" will have true understanding concerning these days. The Word clearly states, *"And it shall come to pass in the last days, saith God, I will pour out of my Spirit upon all flesh: and your sons and your daughters shall prophesy, and your young men shall see visions, and your old men shall dream dreams: And on my servants and on my handmaidens I will pour out in those days of my Spirit; and they shall prophesy"* (Acts 2:17-18).

We read a very amazing and hard to understand account in Revelation 22:8-9, *"And I John saw these things, and heard them. And when I had heard and seen, I fell down to worship before the feet of the angel which shewed me these things. Then saith he unto me, See thou do it not: for I am thy fellowservant, and of thy brethren the prophets, and of them which keep the sayings of this book: worship God."*

I ask you, who gave John all these secret revelations while he was all alone in exile on the Isle of Patmos? Could it possibly have been Daniel? Whoever it was, we know that it was not a member of the Trinity, nor was it an angel, but, as this mysterious messenger, himself said, *"I am thy fellow servant, and of thy brethren, the prophets"*!

This mysterious prophet appeared to Apostle John for the purpose of giving him very in-depth prophecies concerning the last days. He told him about the tribulation that would come upon the earth, the terrible judgments of God upon the nations, the rise of a diabolically evil antichrist who would become a world dictator, the mark of the beast, the final World War (which some call the Battle of Armageddon), the White Throne Judgment, the Holy City, and much more. Who was "that prophet"? Could he have been Daniel who had been commanded by the Lord to *"Shut up the words, and seal the book, even to the time of the end"* (Daniel 12:4)?

Chapter 7

GOD KEEPS HIS SECRETS UNTIL THE RIGHT TIME

I believe there are many great secrets and mysteries of God which have yet to be revealed. In Romans 16:25 we read, *"Now to him that is of power to stablish you according to my gospel, and the preaching of Jesus Christ, according to the revelation of the mystery, which was kept secret since the world began..."*

God keeps His secrets until the right time when they can be revealed. He kept the mystery of salvation through His Son hidden for four thousand years. When you and I walk with God we can keep His secrets too. But the day will come when He will release us to share them, even as He did through Apostle Paul. Nearly two thousand years have passed since Paul was released to reveal the mystery of the Gospel. Now we have come again to the revealing of new truths — end-time truths. The veil between earth and Heaven is becoming thinner and thinner. Our eyes are being enlightened that we might know the mysteries of the eternal ages.

"I CAN'T TELL YOU"

To keep a secret doesn't only mean to keep from speaking, it could also mean that you have to put on an act, or pretend in a way that will throw the enemy into confusion. You don't need to fall in a trap that the enemies of Jesus try to make for you. You don't need to give an answer to every question that is put before you. You can just say, "I can't tell you," like Jesus did many times when the Pharisees interrogated him. And you do not need to make any excuses for your silence. There are many ways of answering those who will get us into trouble. The enemy doesn't need to know the secrets of God. Don't give the devil any information that belongs to God!

MICHAL SAVED DAVID'S LIFE BY PRETENCE

In 1 Samuel 19:11-17, we read the dramatic story how Michal saved the life of her husband, David. I believe God showed her what to do so that she could give him time to escape out of the hands of her father, King Saul, who, because of his mad jealousy and rage, wanted to kill David. When Saul sent his spies to spy on him, planning to kill him in the morning, Michal warned him, *"If thou save not thy life tonight, tomorrow thou shalt be slain. So she let David down through a window and he went, and fled, and escaped. And [she] took an image, and laid it in the bed, and put a pillow of goats' hair for his bolster, and covered it with a cloth."* When Saul's messenger tried to arrest David, she told them that he was sick. When they reported this to Saul, he ordered them to go and *"Bring him up to me in the bed, that I may slay him."* And when they returned to get him, they discovered that instead of it being David, it was an image hiding under the covers. Saul was filled with anger.

When Saul interrogated his daughter, in order to save her life, she told him that David had begged her to let him escape or he would have killed her. It wasn't quite the truth, but what else could she have said? Her father would have killed her too! By pretending that David was sick in bed she gave him time to escape from certain death.

There may come a time when we will have to hide someone or save another person's life. God will let you know how to do it so that you can deliver that one from torture or death without sinning.

ABIGAIL SAVES THE LIVES OF HER FAMILY BY DECEIVING HER HUSBAND

This is one of my favourite Bible stories. It is recorded in the twenty-fifth chapter of 1 Samuel. In this story, David and his men are hiding from King Saul in the Wilderness of Paran. There was a very wealthy man in that area by the name of Nabal who was a big "rancher." He had three thousand sheep and one thousand goats, so that gives us an idea of how rich he was.

The Bible says that his wife Abigail was a woman of good understanding and a beautiful countenance, but he was churlish and evil. David was in need of food for his followers, so he sent ten men to the "ranch" to ask for assistance to feed them. David sent a message of goodwill and told how they had protected Nabal's shepherds during the time that they were out in the fields with their herds. He asked a "love offering" in return. He said, *"Let the young men find favour in thine eyes, for we come in a good day, give, I pray thee, whatsoever cometh to thine hand unto thy servants, and to thy son, David"* (verse 8).

However, when Nabal heard their request he became angry, and insulted David. "Who is David?" he asked, mockingly. He added that there were many rebels in the land who had broken away from their masters, and, *"why should I take my bread, and my water, and my flesh, that I have killed for my shearers, and give it unto men whom I know not whence they be?"* (verse 11).

When David received this report, he became angry and determined to retaliate, telling the men to gird on their swords. David had six hundred men; four hundred were going to make a raid on Nabal's "ranch."

It was then that one of Nabal's servants told Abigail what had happened, and warned her to prepare herself because they were sure to be raided by David and his men, and that not one would be left alive. He said that David and his men had been good to them, and they had protected them, and that the two groups had enjoyed good fellowship together in the fields. He added, *"Our master...is such a son of Belial, that a man cannot speak to him"* (verse 17).

When Abigail heard this, she immediately gave orders to prepare bread, wine, sheep, corn, raisins, and figs, to take to David. She sent them on ahead, as she got herself ready to follow on her donkey to meet David. The Bible says clearly, *"But she told not her husband Nabal"* (verse 19b). When she met David, she got off her donkey, fell before him, bowing down to the ground, and begged him, *"Upon me, my lord, upon me let this iniquity be: and let thine handmaid, I pray thee, speak in thine audience, and hear the words of thine handmaid. Let not my lord, I pray thee, regard this man of Belial, even Nabal: for as his name is, so is he; Nabal is his name, and folly is with him: but I thine handmaid saw not the young men of my lord, whom thou didst send. Now therefore, my lord, as the LORD liveth, and as thy soul liveth, seeing the LORD hath withholden thee from coming to shed blood, and from avenging thyself with thine own hand, now let thine enemies, and they that seek evil to my lord, be as Nabal. And now this blessing which thine handmaid hath brought unto my lord, let it even be given unto the young men that follow my lord. I pray thee, forgive the trespass of thine handmaid: for the LORD will certainly make my lord a sure house; because my lord fighteth the battles of the LORD, and evil hath not been found in thee all thy days. Yet a man is risen to pursue thee, and to seek thy soul: but the soul of my lord shall be bound in the bundle of life with the LORD thy God; and the souls of thine enemies, them shall he sling out, as out of the middle of a sling. And it shall come to pass, when the LORD shall have done to my lord according to all the good that he hath spoken concerning thee, and shall have appointed thee ruler over Israel; That this shall be no grief unto thee, nor offence of heart unto my lord, either that thou hast shed blood causeless, or that my lord hath avenged himself: but when the LORD shall have dealt well with my lord, then remember thine handmaid"* (1 Samuel 25:24-31).

When Abigail received the information about her husband's actions, she didn't ask herself, "What will Nabal do to save our lives?" Instead, she immediately, began to secretly make plans how she herself would spare their lives. She was a woman of great wisdom. She knew there was no use in talking to her husband. He was a "churlish" man. That means he was surly and rude. One cannot reason with such a person. The name Nabal means "fool."

What are you going to do when you are married to a fool? You, yourself, must take responsibility for what should be done. She knew their lives were in danger. Abigail saved Nabal's life, even though he didn't deserve it, for her plea touched the heart of David and he answered her, *"Blessed be the LORD God of Israel, which sent thee this day to meet me: And blessed be thy advice, and blessed be thou, which hast kept me this day from coming to shed blood, and from avenging myself with mine own hand. For in very deed, as the LORD God of Israel liveth, which hath kept me back from hurting thee, except thou hadst hasted and come to meet me, surely there had not been left unto Nabal by the morning light any that pisseth against the wall"* (1 Samuel 25:32-34).

The greatness of God was in Abigail because she took the blame for her husband's evil deeds. It was only because she was able to keep her actions secret from her husband that she was able to deliver her family and household. By keeping God's secret Abigail was able to save lives, including Nabal's.

HEZEKIAH'S TERRIBLE MISTAKE

Sometimes, we like to brag about the great things God has done for us or through us. We may even think we are giving honour to Him. But it is not always a good thing for the enemy to hear about that which will make him jealous of us, and our successes.

After the King of Babylon heard about King Hezekiah's miraculous healing he sent messengers with a complimentary letter and a present. Hezekiah was so flattered by these important visitors that he *"showed them the house of his precious things, the silver, and the gold, and the spices, and the precious ointment, and all the house of his armour, and all that was found in his treasures: there was nothing in his house, nor in all his dominion, that Hezekiah showed them not"* (Isaiah 39:2).

When the prophet Isaiah heard what he had done, he was grieved, because he knew that Hezekiah had made a foolish mistake. He immediately sent him the word of the Lord, warning him, *"Behold, the days come, that all that is in thine house, and that which thy fathers have laid up in store until this day, shall be carried to Babylon: nothing shall be left, saith the LORD. And of thy sons that shall issue from thee, which thou shalt beget, shall they take away; and they shall be eunuchs in the palace of the king of Babylon"* (Isaiah 39:6-7).

Americans have been doing that for a long time, we have been showing many of our secrets to the spies of nations that hate us. The enemy knows our strength and our weakness. He knows how vulnerable we are for attack. God is trying to tell us to use wisdom.

Sometimes its even wrong to show our treasures to one who is not an enemy.

I remember when I first arrived in Shanghai I was very naive, as a new missionary always is. I left my good fountain pen in the sitting room when I retired to my bedroom. The next morning, as we missionaries were sitting together in the sitting room, one of them picked up my pen and asked, "Who does this belong to?" I acknowledged that it was mine. He gave me a warning I never forgot. "Never let things like this lie around, because if you do, you will be tempting the natives. They love pens, and other precious things like that, and they are too poor to afford them, so it tempts them to steal them." Since then, I have always tried to be careful not to "tempt the natives." Even a good person can fall because of temptation.

There are many ways in which we can tempt people or cause them to become discontent with their lifestyle. If God is giving you extra money, don't go around bragging about it to the one who has none. And don't try to make them feel "little" or "sinful" because they have less, or because you think they don't have "your faith" for finances. Always try to be modest in every way.

God wants us to be wise in many ways concerning the Kingdom of God. We have many braggarts and boasters; and not a few are in the ministry! I believe God is calling us to be extra wise in these days. We are really going to have to be careful about the things we share with others.

Some of you will be called, like Joseph, to store up certain things for the days ahead. Be careful to whom you reveal this type of ministry. Don't show every one your "granaries." Hezekiah couldn't keep God's secret. He was "bought" with a present. There always will be those who can be "bought" with a present, or with flattery. Satan always has those who will pretend to be your friend, but whose intentions towards you are evil. And if you do not have discernment they will deceive you. Always be careful that you are not distracted by a decoy that satan has put in your pathway. God wants us to be wise as serpents and harmless as doves.

Chapter 8

MARY HID THE SECRETS OF GOD IN HER HEART

When the shepherd told Mary about the angels and the message they had brought them from heaven, the Bible says, *"Mary kept all these things, and pondered them in her heart"* (Luke 2:19).

She did not go around bragging about her great "miracle experience." She kept these things in her heart and she pondered over them. She didn't even ask her rabbi about all that had happened.

Sometimes there are things that you just to have to keep in your heart, and ponder over, and wonder about. Mary also kept the prophecy old Simeon gave them when Jesus was dedicated to the Lord in the Temple.

The devil will say if you don't confess the Lord before men then God will not confess you in Heaven. Confession is one thing; ministering about Jesus Christ is one thing, but going around telling about these secrets of God is another thing. Jesus warned us, *"Give not that which is holy unto the dogs, neither cast ye your pearls before swine, lest they trample them under their feet, and turn again and rend you"* (Matthew 7:6). We must not take the precious jewels that God has given us, and share them with those who are unclean. In the Bible swine were called unclean by God. When Jesus says that we should not give the holy things to the swine, He means that we should not give the holy, dedicated things of God, to that which is profane. Don't inform the devil of the secrets of God; keep the secrets of God in your heart.

Jesus said, in John 16:12, *"I have yet many things to say unto you, but ye cannot bear them now."* Jesus knew that if He would tell His disciples all the things that He would have liked to have told them, that the deeper truths would have been a stumbling block for them. It would have destroyed their faith, because they were so immature in their understanding concerning the things of God

God wants us to grow into maturity. With every secret comes the burden of responsibility. The truths of God and the secrets of God are a very great weight to carry.

SECRET ESCAPE

In times when our lives are in danger, we might have to escape like baby Moses escaped — in a basket (Exodus 2:2-10). In Acts 9:25 we read how Paul escaped from men who had plans to kill him in Damascus when he was let down the wall in a basket.

In order to escape from the angry crowd, Jesus was able to make Himself invisible (Luke 4:30, John 8:59). When they tried to arrest Jesus, He suddenly disappeared. He didn't allow Himself to be taken. He didn't submit to their man-made authority to arrest him. Sometimes fear can paralyze you. You don't need to submit to the devil to arrest you. If there is no way of escape, you have to submit, but if you can escape, do it.

THE FAITHFUL KEEP SECRETS — THE UNFAITHFUL DON'T

God wants us to be wise. Proverbs 11:13 states, *"A talebearer revealeth secrets: but he that is of a faithful spirit concealeth the matter."*

God needs people with faithful spirits who will be able to conceal the King's business in these latter days. Be careful of those who gossip about others. Remember, *"He that goeth about as a talebearer revealeth secrets: therefore meddle not with him that flattereth with his lips"* (Proverbs 20:19). *"Confidence in an unfaithful man in time of trouble is like a broken tooth, and a foot out of joint"* (Proverbs 25:19).

We know that Proverbs 3:32 says, *"His secret is with the righteous."* Your faithfulness in keeping God's secrets will be in your eternal records as recorded by the angels of the Lord. If you want to be counted as a righteous one in God's sight, you must learn to keep His secrets. He will surely reveal to you the secrets He knows you will keep. To be found faithful and righteous in His sight means you have gained His trust, and He will continue to share with you the secrets of His heart.

Chapter 9

**LOVE IS THE KEY TO BEING ABLE
TO KEEP A SECRET**

The only way that we can have the strength to keep a secret is through love. Love covers a multitude of sins. We are living in a time of accusation, betrayal, distrust, and self-promotion. We need wisdom and discernment to know what is right and what is wrong. I believe that we have come to a day when the Lord is going to give His children greater wisdom and discernment than we have ever had before.

Remember that by covering another person's sins, you may be saving that one's life, and that in saving one life, you could be saving your own!

There are two kinds of secrets. One is the secret of knowing another person's weakness or failures, and being able to keep it between yourself and God alone. It is wrong to spread it about. Remember again what David wrote when Saul was killed; even though Saul was his deadly enemy, he still did not give an evil report against him. He tried to cover Saul's wrong doings and his weakness. He said, *"Tell it not in Gath, publish it not in the streets of Askelon; lest the daughters of the Philistines rejoice, lest the daughters of the uncircumcised triumph"* (2 Samuel 1:20).

When my father died of cancer, the doctor warned me that he would suffer great agony before he passed away. But one hour later he quietly "fell asleep in Jesus." When I asked the Father how was it that he could pass without enduring great pain, He told me, "Your father never caused others to suffer, so I spared him pain." It was true. My father never gossiped nor repeated someone else's failures and wrongs to anyone, even my mother. He just never talked about people in an unkind way. Because he was kind to others, God was kind to him. He had a good heart. A good heart covers the wrongs of the bad-hearted person.

The second kind of secret is the ability to keep in one's heart the things which God reveals to you, but which are forbidden to others. Paul said that when he was caught up into Paradise, he *"heard unspeakable words, which it is not lawful for a man to utter"* (2 Corinthians 12:4). Paul knew the importance of keeping God's secrets.

My friend, Valerie, shared a dream with me, which I would like to share with you.

"In a dream I saw a huge cardinal on my screened-in patio. It was the size of an eagle, and brilliant red. It sang glorious melodies that took me into the Presence of God. I was so happy and ecstatic that I wanted to share it with my son. I called up the stairs, 'Timothy, come quickly! See this marvelous thing.' I then ran out onto the patio, and brushed the cardinal's belly so he could hop onto my arm. Instead of hopping on, he bit into my arm with his beak, and the pain shot through me. I tried to shake him off, but he wouldn't let go. The pain was growing so great, I banged him against the post. He fell off. Timothy then walked in and said, 'Mom, why did you call me to see a dead bird?' The bird's colors had faded and now he seemed small. I awoke instantly in great distress.

"After three days of fasting and praying, the Lord spoke to my heart and told me the secret things belong to the Lord, and He wanted to share His secrets with me, but I had to learn to keep His secrets and only share them with those He told me, and some secrets were to be shared with no one. He said that not everyone was ready for them. He said they would take a pure and holy thing, and mock it, and call it 'dead' or 'ugly.' Others would destroy what He was trying to build in me, and use through me. He told me the secret things belong to the Lord, and He reveals them to whom He wills. We need to use wisdom, and share only what He permits, and when He allows it."

Be wise, beloved, and the Lord will reveal to you many wonderful secrets which He has kept secret from the foundation of this world. If you cannot understand some of the things the Holy Spirit has spoken to you, just keep it in your heart, and ponder it, like Mary did. In God's time you will understand.

CLOSING PRAYER

Father, You have called some of Your servants into ministries which must be done in secret, for if they were to talk about their "work" they would endanger the lives of their fellow men. Help us to be faithful. Give us the grace to take "the vow of silence" so that people can come to us with their problems, their convictions, and trust us with the deepest, darkest sins of their lives, knowing that we will take it no further than the Throne of God in secret prayer.

Please, O God, give me the Grace of God, so that I will be able to control my tongue, for I honestly confess that it is the member of my body which transgresses the most readily. Help me to be like Jesus, Who was able to hide His heart's secrets even from those who were His nearest and dearest. If you can trust me, I know I will be lifted into a higher dimension than I have ever been in before. AMEN!

Gwen R. Shaw

More Life-Changing Books

GWEN SHAW'S AUTOBIOGRAPHY

UNCONDITIONAL SURRENDER. The life story of Gwen R. Shaw, lovingly known as "Sister Gwen" to thousands of people in over one hundred nations. You will laugh and cry with her as you feel the heartbeat of a great woman of God who has given all to Him, asking only for souls in return. Your life will be challenged as you walk with her through mission field after mission field. You will never be the same when you read how God pours out His Spirit and confirms His Word. Paperback ....#000101 $15.00
Video NTSC (North American format) ....#GSL-99 $20.00
Video PAL (European format) ....#GSLP-99 $20.00

DAILY DEVOTIONALS BY GWEN SHAW

DAILY PREPARATIONS FOR PERFECTION — This daily devotional comes to you exactly as the Holy Spirit spoke to the author's heart in her own private devotions. You will feel that Jesus is speaking to you every time you open it. It is loved by all. You'll read it and re-read it ....Paperback #000202 $12.50

DAY BY DAY— This daily devotional book based on the Psalms will give you an inspiring word directly from the Throne Room each day to fill your heart with praise to God. Starting each day with praise is the secret of a joy-filled life ....Softcover #000204 $9.95
....Hardcover #000203 $18.50
Also available in French ....Hardcover #000203FR $18.50

FROM THE HEART OF JESUS — This devotional book will take you back to Bible days and you will walk and talk with Jesus and His disciples as he ministered to the people, as He suffered and died and as He rose again from the dead. These words from the heart of Jesus will go straight to your heart, bringing comfort, peace, encouragement and hope! 923 pages ....Hardcover #000207 $29.95

GEMS OF WISDOM — *A daily devotional based on the book of Proverbs.* In the Proverbs you will find instruction for upright living, honesty, justice and wisdom. Every word in the Proverbs applies to today's problems as when they were first written. If you are going through great difficulties and facing problems which seem to have no solution, you will find the answer in these Proverbs. You'll have a Proverb and an inspired writing about it for each day of the year! A great gift idea for graduates and newlyweds! ....Hardcover #000209 $25.95

IN THE BEGINNING — *A daily devotional based on the book of Genesis.* The Book of Genesis is perhaps the most important book in the Old Testament. It is the foundation stone of all knowledge and wisdom. Deep and wonderful truths hidden in the pages of Genesis are revealed in this devotional book. You'll be amazed at the soul-stirring writings inspired by the well-known stories of Genesis. Hardcover .... #000211 $27.95

DEEPEN YOUR WALK WITH GOD WITH CLASSIC ANOINTED BIBLE STUDIES BY GWEN SHAW!

BEHOLD THE BRIDEGROOM COMETH! A Bible study on the soon return of Jesus Christ. With so many false teachings these days, it is important that we realize how imminent the rapture of the saints of God really is .... #000304 $6.50

 ENDUED WITH LIGHT TO REIGN FOREVER. This deeply profound Bible study reveals the characteristics of the eternal, supernatural, creative light of God as found in His Word. The "Father of Lights," created man in His image. He longs for man to step out of darkness and into His light .... #000306 $5.00

GOD'S END-TIME BATTLE-PLAN. This study on spiritual warfare gives you the biblical weapons for spiritual warfare such as victory through dancing, shouting, praising, uplifted hands, marching, etc. It has been a great help to many who have been bound by tradition. .... #000305 $8.00

 IT'S TIME FOR REVIVAL. A Bible study on revival that not only gives scriptural promises of the end-time revival, but also presents the stories of revivals in the past and the revivalists whom God used. It will stir your heart and encourage you to believe for great revival! .... #000311 $7.75

OUR MINISTERING ANGELS. A scriptural Bible study on the topic of angels. Angels will be playing a more and more prominent part in these last days. We need to understand about them and their ministry. Read exciting accounts of angelic help .... #000308 $7.50

POUR OUT YOUR HEART. A wonderful Bible study on travailing prayer. The hour has come to intercede before the throne of God. The call to intercession is for everyone, and we must carry the Lord's burden and weep for the lost so that the harvest can be brought in quickly..#000301 $5.00

REDEEMING THE LAND. A Bible study on spiritual warfare. This important teaching will help you know your authority through the Blood of Jesus to dislodge evil spirits, break the curse, and restore God's blessing upon the land. ....#000309 $9.50

THE FINE LINE. This Bible study clearly magnifies the "fine line" of difference between the soul realm and the spirit realm. Both are intangible and therefore cannot be discerned with the five senses, but must be discerned by the Holy Spirit and the Word of God. A must for the deeper Christian..#000307 $6.00

THE POWER OF THE PRECIOUS BLOOD. A Bible study on the Blood of Jesus. The author shares how it was revealed to her how much Satan fears Jesus' Blood. This Bible study will help you overcome and destroy the works of Satan in your life and the lives of loved ones! ....#000303 $5.00

THE POWER OF PRAISE. When God created the heavens and the earth, He was surrounded by praise. Miracles happen when holy people praise a Holy God! Praise is the language of creation. If prayer can move the hand of God, how much more praise can move Him! ....#000312 $5.00

YE SHALL RECEIVE POWER FROM ON HIGH. This is a much needed foundational teaching on the Baptism of the Holy Spirit. It will enable you to teach this subject, as well as to understand these truths more fully yourself ....#000310 $5.00

YOUR APPOINTMENT WITH GOD. A Bible study on fasting. Fasting is one of the most neglected sources of power over bondages of Satan that God has given the Church. The author's experiences shared in this Bible study will change your life ....#000302 $5.00

IN-DEPTH BIBLE STUDIES FOR THE SERIOUS STUDENT OF GOD'S WORD

FORGIVE AND RECEIVE. This Bible Study is a lesson to the church on the much-needed truths of forgiveness and restoration. The epistle to Philemon came from the heart of Paul who had experienced great forgiveness ....#000406 $7.00

GRACE ALONE. This study teaches the reader to gain freedom in the finished work of the Cross by forsaking works (which cannot add to salvation) and live by *Grace Alone*..............#000402 $13.00

MYSTERY REVEALED. Search the depths of God's riches in one of Paul's most profound epistles, "to the praise of His glory!" Learn the "mystery" of the united Body of Christ..#000403 $15.00

OUR GLORIOUS HEAD. This book teaches vital truths for today, assisting the reader in discerning false teachings, when the philosophies of men are being promoted as being the truths of God. Jesus Christ is the Head of His Body! ....#000404 $9.00

THE CATCHING AWAY! This is a very timely Bible study because Jesus is coming soon! The book of 1 Thessalonians explains God's revelation to Paul on the rapture of the saints. 2 Thessalonians reveals what will happen after the rapture when the antichrist takes over...#000407 $13.00

THE LOVE LETTER. This expository study of the letter to the first church of Europe will give the reader an understanding of Paul's great love for the church that was born out of his suffering. ....#000405 $9.00

POPULAR BIBLE COURSE

THE TRIBES OF ISRAEL. This popular and well-loved study on the thirteen tribes of Israel will show you your place in the spiritual tribes in these last days. Understand yourself and others better through the study of this Bible Course!
...................#000501 $45.00 • Set of 13 tapes #TGS1 $42.00

THE WOMEN OF THE BIBLE SERIES BY GWEN SHAW,

opens a window into the lives of the women of the Bible in the style of historical novels. Their joys and heartaches were the same as ours today.

 EVE—MOTHER OF US ALL. Read the life story of the first woman. Discover the secrets of one of the most neglected and misunderstood stories in history..#000801 $4.50

SARAH—PRINCESS OF ALL MANKIND. She was beautiful — and barren. Feel the heartbeat and struggles of this woman who left so great an impact on us all..#000802 $4.50

 REBEKAH—THE BRIDE. The destiny of the world was determined when she said three simple words, "I will go!" Enjoy this touching story. ....#000803 $4.50

LEAH AND RACHEL—THE TWIN WIVES OF JACOB. You will feel their dreams, their pains, their jealousies and their love for one man. ....#000804 $4.50

 MIRIAM—THE PROPHETESS. Miriam was the first female to lead worship, the first woman to whom the Lord gave the title "Leader of God's people."..#000805 $7.50

OTHER BOOKS BY GWEN SHAW

GOING HOME. This book is a treasure which answers so many questions and comforts so many hearts. It gives strength and faith, and helps one to cope with the pain of the loss of a loved one. This book is not really a book about dying, but about Going Home to our Eternal Abode with our loving Heavenly Father......................#000607 $8.00

 LOVE, THE LAW OF THE ANGELS. This is undoubtedly the greatest of Gwen Shaw's writings. It carries a message of healing and life in a sad and fallen civilization. Love heals the broken-hearted and sets disarray in order. You will never be the same after reading this beautiful book about love. ....#000601 $10.00

SONG OF LOVE. She was a heart-broken missionary, far from home. She cried out to God for help. He spoke, "Turn to the Song of Solomon and read!" As she turned in obedience, the Lord took her into the "Throne Room" of Heaven and taught her about the love of Christ for His Bride, the church. She fell in love with Jesus afresh, and you will too ....#000401 $7.50

THE FALSE FAST. Now, from the pen of Gwen Shaw, author of Your Appointment With God (a Bible Study on fasting), comes an exposé on the False Fast. It will help you to examine your motives for fasting, and make your foundations sure, so that your fast will be a potent tool in the hands of God......................................#000602 $2.50

THE LIGHT WILL COME FROM RUSSIA. The thrilling testimony of Mother Barbara, Abbess of the Mount of Olives in Jerusalem. She shares prophecies which were given to her concerning the nations of the world in our time by a holy bishop of the Kremlin, ten days before his death just prior to the Russian Revolution ....#000606 $5.50

 THE PARABLE OF THE GOLDEN RAIN. This is the story of how revivals come and go, and a true picture, in parable language, of how the Church tries to replace the genuine move of the Spirit with man-made programs and tactics. It's amusing and convicting at the same time ....#000603 $4.00

THEY SHALL MOUNT UP WITH WINGS AS EAGLES. Though you may feel old or tired, if you wait on the Lord, you shall mount up on wings as eagles! Let this book encourage you to stretch your wings and fulfill your destiny — no matter what your age! ....#000604 $6.95

 TO BE LIKE JESUS. Based on her Throne Room experience in 1971, the author shares the Father's heart about our place as sons in His Family. Nothing is more important than To Be Like Jesus! ....#000605 $6.95

POCKET SERMON BOOKS BY GWEN SHAW

BEHOLD, THIS DREAMER COMETH. Dreams and dreamers are God's gift to humanity to bring His purposes into the hearts of mankind. The life of Joseph, the dreamer, will encourage you to believe God to fulfill the dream He has put into your heart ....#000707 $2.00

 BREAKTHROUGH. Just like when Peter was in prison, sometimes you need a "breakthrough" in your life! This book reveals the truth in a fresh and living way! ....#000708 $2.00

DON'T STRIKE THE ROCK! When Moses became angry with the people's rebellion and disobeyed God's order to speak to the Rock, it cost him his entrance into the Promised Land. Don't allow anything to keep you from fulfilling God's perfect will for your life!..........#000704 $2.00

GOD WILL DESTROY THE VEIL OF BLINDNESS. "...as the veil of the Temple was rent...I shall again rend the veil in two....for...the Arab, so they shall know that I am God...." This was the word of the Lord concerning God's plan for the nations in the days to come. Join in with Abraham's prayer "Let Ishmael live before Thee!"................#000712 $2.00

HASTENING OUR REDEMPTION. All of Heaven and Earth are waiting for the Body of Christ to rise up in maturity and reclaim what we lost in the Fall of Man. Applying the Blood of Jesus is the key to *Hastening Our Redemption* ....#000705 $1.50

 IT CAN BE AVERTED. Many people today are burdened and fearful over prophecies of doom and destruction. However, the Bible is clear that God prefers mercy over judgment when His people humble themselves and pray..#000706 $2.00

KAIROS TIME. That once in a lifetime opportunity—that second, or minute, or hour, or year, or even longer, when a golden opportunity is sovereignly given to us by the Almighty. What we do with it can change our lives and possibly even change the world...................#000709 $1.50

 KNOWING ONE ANOTHER IN THE SPIRIT. Experience great peace as you learn to understand the difficulties your friends, enemies and loved ones face that help to form their character. "Wherefore henceforth know we no man after the flesh..." (II Cor. 5:16a) ....#000703 $2.00

THE ANOINTING BREAKS THE YOKE. Learn how the anointing of God can set you free from your bondage: free to fulfill your destiny in the call of God on your life!...#000710 $1.50

 THE CRUCIFIED LIFE. When you suffer, knowing the cause is not your own sin, for you have searched your heart before God, then you must accept that it is God doing a new thing in your life. Let joy rise up within you because you are a partaker of Christ's suffering ....#000701 $2.00

THE MASTER IS COME AND CALLETH FOR THEE. Read about how the Lord called Gwen Shaw to begin the ministry of the End-Time Handmaidens and Servants. Perhaps the Master is also calling you into His service. Bring Him the fragments of your life — He will put them together again. An anointed message booklet ....#000702 $2.00

 THE MERCY SEAT. The Days of Grace are coming to a close, and the Days of Mercy are now here. And oh, how we need mercy! There never has been a time when we needed it more!................#000711 $2.00

CHILDREN'S BOOKS BY GWEN SHAW

LITTLE ONES TO HIM BELONG. Based on the testimonies of children's visions of Heaven and the death of a small Chinese boy, Sister Gwen weaves a delightful story of the precious joys of Heaven for children of all ages ....#000901 $9.00

TELL ME THE STORIES OF JESUS. Some of the greatest New Testament stories of the Life of Jesus and written in a way that will interest children and help them to love Jesus............#000902 $9.00

BOOKS ABOUT HEAVEN

INTRA MUROS — Rebecca Springer. One of the most beautiful books about Heaven is available here in its unabridged form. Read the glorious account of this ordinary believer's visit to Heaven. It brings great comfort to the bereaved ....#109101 $8.00

PARADISE, THE HOLY CITY AND THE GLORY OF THE THRONE — Elwood Scott. Visited by a saint of God who spent forty days in Heaven, Elwood Scott's detailed description will edify and comfort your heart. Especially good for those with lost loved ones. Look into Heaven!..#104201 $8.00

PROPHECIES AND VISIONS

THE DAY OF THE LORD IS NEAR: Vol. I - IV. *"Surely the Lord GOD will do nothing, but he revealeth his secret unto his servants the prophets."* (Amos 3:7) A collection of prophecies, visions and dreams. This startling compilation will help you understand what God has in His heart for the near future. ....Each Volume $10.00 • Volumes I - IV with binder..#001000 $25.00

BOOKS PUBLISHED BY ENGELTAL PRESS

ATTITUDES IN THE BEATITUDES — Esther Rollins. An instructor of the Word of God for 50 years, Esther taught this anointed course on the Beatitudes as a guest teacher at our School of Ministry. Both basic and profound, this dynamic teaching is full of insight for the Christian walk ....#098801 $5.95

BANISHED FOR FAITH — Emil Waltner. The stirring story of the courageous forefathers of Gwen Shaw, the Hutterite Mennonites, who were banished from their homeland and suffered great persecution for their faith. Republished with an index and epilogue by Gwen Shaw. ....#126201 $12.95

BECOMING A SERVANT — Robert Baldwin. Learn what is on God's heart about servanthood. We must learn to serve before we can be trusted to lead. If you want to be great in God's Kingdom, learn to be the servant of all..#006901 $2.00

 FIVE STONES AND A SWORD — Gene Little. Read the true account of how Jesus is appearing to His lost children, and revealing Himself to these sons of Abraham. Your heart will leap with joy, and you will be encouraged, with new faith, that God will send a great revival among the Moslem people of the world..#072501 #1.50

FOOTPRINTS — Larry Hunt. A collection of poems and stories reflecting the hand of God upon this humble pastor during 35 years of ministry...#057901 $3.75

 FROM DUST TO GLORY — June Lewis. The Lord intends more than just salvation for us. He is making vessels of eternal Glory if we submit to Him. Rise up from your dust!........................#072001 $7.50

HOLY ANN — Helen Bingham. This humble Irish woman moved the arm of God through simple faith and prevailing prayer. Read these modern miracles that are told like a story from the Old Testament. The record of a lifetime of answered prayer ....#010501 $4.95

 IT WAS WORTH IT ALL — Elly Matz. The story of a beautiful woman whose courage will inspire you. Feel her heart as she tells of her starving father, the young Communist engineer she married, the villages mysteriously evacuated, the invading German army, the concentration camp where she was a prisoner, and her escape into freedom ....#078001 $5.95

LET'S KEEP MOVING — Pete Snyder. Travel with Peter to Haiti where he struggles with the call of God to be a missionary. Identify with Peter's growth of faith through trials and tribulations as he travels on to China where new adventures await and faithful endurance is needed. A must for the called! ....#108801 $9.95

RULING IN THEIR MIDST — June Lewis. The Lord has called us to rule even in the midst of all demonic activity and Satan's plans and schemes. Sister June has learned spiritual warfare from the Lord Himself, *"who teacheth my hands to war,"* in the face of personal tragedy
....#072002 $6.00

Prices are subject to change.

For a complete catalogue with current pricing, contact:

Engeltal Press
P.O. Box 447
Jasper, ARK 72641 U.S.A.
Telephone (870) 446-2665
Fax (870) 446-2259
Email books@eth-s.org
Website www.engeltalpress.com